30 EASY Celtic Guitar SOLOS

Arranged by
MARK PHILLIPS

Guitar performed by Doug Boduch

ISBN 978-1-4803-5266-7

HAL•LEONARD®

Visit Hal Leonard Online at
www.halleonard.com

Contact us:
Hal Leonard
7777 West Bluemound Road
Milwaukee, WI 53213
Email: info@halleonard.com

In Europe, contact:
Hal Leonard Europe Limited
42 Wigmore Street
Marylebone, London, W1U 2RN
Email: info@halleonardeurope.com

In Australia, contact:
Hal Leonard Australia Pty. Ltd.
4 Lentara Court
Cheltenham, Victoria, 3192 Australia
Email: info@halleonard.com.au

Contents

The Ash Grove

Old Welsh Air

Boulavogue

Irish Folk Song
Words and Music by P. J. McCall

Blind Mary

By Turlough O'Carolan

Track 2

Moderately

Carolan's Cap

By Turlough O'Carolan

Track 4

Moderately

Carolan's Draught

Track 5

By Turlough O'Carolan

Moderately

Carrickfergus

Track 6

Traditional Irish Folk Song

Down by the Sally Gardens

Track 11

Traditional Irish Folk Song

Moderately, in 2

Castle of Dromore

Traditional Irish Folk Song

Cliffs of Doneen

Traditional Irish Folk Song

Track 8

Moderately

The Curragh of Kildare

Track 9

Traditional Irish Folk Song

Moderately slow, in 2

19

Danny Boy

Track 10

Words by Frederick Edward Weatherly
Traditioinal Irish Folk Melody

Moderately slow

John O'Connor

Track 12

By Turlough O'Carolan

Moderately, in 2

Kathleen Mavourneen

Track 13

Words and Music by
Frederick N. Crouch

Moderately

A Lark in the Clear Air

Track 14

Words and Music by
Sir Samuel Ferguson

Moderately slow

Loch Lomond

Track 15

Scottish Folk Song

Moderately, in 2

To Coda ⊕

Minstrel Boy

Track 16

Traditional

Moderately

Molly Malone

(Cockles and Mussels)

Irish Folk Song

Mountains of Mourne

Words by Percy French
Traditional Irish Melody

Track 18

My Love Is Like a Red, Red Rose

Traditional Folk Melody
Lyrics by Robert Burns

Track 19

D.S. al Coda

⊕ **Coda**

Niel Gow's Lament

Track 20

By Niel Gow

Moderately slow, in 2

Planxty Irwin

Track 21

By Turlough O'Carolan

Moderately slow, in 2

The Trees They Do Grow High

Track 27

Traditional

Moderately fast

The Rose of Allendale

Track 22

Traditional Irish Folk Song

Moderately fast

The Rose of Mooncoin

Track 23

Traditional Irish Folk Song

Moderately fast

The Rose of Tralee

Words by C. Mordaunt Spencer
Music by Charles W. Glover

Track 24

Moderately

Skye Boat Song

Traditional

Track 25

Moderately

4th time, to Coda ⊕

2nd time, D. S. al Coda
(take repeat)

⊕ Coda

The Star of the County Down

Track 26

Celtic Folk Song

Moderately, in 2

*Strum downward with backs of nails.

The Water Is Wide

Track 28

Traditional

Ye Banks and Braes o' Bonnie Doon

Track 30

Lyrics by Robert Burns
Melody by Charles Miller

Moderately slow, in 2

Wild Mountain Thyme

Track 29

Traditional Scottish Folk Song

Moderately

EASY GUITAR WITH NOTES & TAB

This series features simplified arrangements with notes, tab, chord charts, and strum and pick patterns.

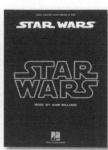

MIXED FOLIOS

00702287	Acoustic	$16.99
00702002	Acoustic Rock Hits for Easy Guitar	$15.99
00702166	All-Time Best Guitar Collection	$19.99
00702232	Best Acoustic Songs for Easy Guitar	$14.99
00119835	Best Children's Songs	$16.99
00702233	Best Hard Rock Songs	$15.99
00703055	The Big Book of Nursery Rhymes & Children's Songs	$16.99
00698978	Big Christmas Collection	$17.99
00702394	Bluegrass Songs for Easy Guitar	$12.99
00289632	Bohemian Rhapsody	$17.99
00703387	Celtic Classics	$14.99
00224808	Chart Hits of 2016-2017	$14.99
00267383	Chart Hits of 2017-2018	$14.99
00334293	Chart Hits of 2019-2020	$16.99
00702149	Children's Christian Songbook	$9.99
00702028	Christmas Classics	$8.99
00101779	Christmas Guitar	$14.99
00702185	Christmas Hits	$10.99
00702141	Classic Rock	$8.95
00159642	Classical Melodies	$12.99
00253933	Disney/Pixar's Coco	$16.99
00702203	CMT's 100 Greatest Country Songs	$29.99
00702283	The Contemporary Christian Collection	$16.99
00196954	Contemporary Disney	$19.99

00702239	Country Classics for Easy Guitar	$22.99
00702257	Easy Acoustic Guitar Songs	$14.99
00702280	Easy Guitar Tab White Pages	$29.99
00702041	Favorite Hymns for Easy Guitar	$10.99
00222701	Folk Pop Songs	$14.99
00126894	Frozen	$14.99
00333922	Frozen 2	$14.99
00702286	Glee	$16.99
00702160	The Great American Country Songbook	$16.99
00267383	Great American Gospel for Guitar	$12.99
00702050	Great Classical Themes for Easy Guitar	$8.99
00702116	Greatest Hymns for Guitar	$10.99
00275088	The Greatest Showman	$17.99
00148030	Halloween Guitar Songs	$14.99
00702273	Irish Songs	$12.99
00192503	Jazz Classics for Easy Guitar	$14.99
00702275	Jazz Favorites for Easy Guitar	$15.99
00702274	Jazz Standards for Easy Guitar	$17.99
00702162	Jumbo Easy Guitar Songbook	$19.99
00232285	La La Land	$16.99
00702258	Legends of Rock	$14.99
00702189	MTV's 100 Greatest Pop Songs	$24.95
00702272	1950s Rock	$15.99
00702271	1960s Rock	$15.99
00702270	1970s Rock	$16.99
00702269	1980s Rock	$15.99

00702268	1990s Rock	$19.99
00109725	Once	$14.99
00702187	Selections from O Brother Where Art Thou?	$19.99
00702178	100 Songs for Kids	$14.99
00702515	Pirates of the Caribbean	$16.99
00702125	Praise and Worship for Guitar	$10.99
00287930	Songs from *A Star Is Born, The Greatest Showman, La La Land*, and More Movie Musicals	$16.99
00702285	Southern Rock Hits	$12.99
00156420	Star Wars Music	$14.99
00121535	30 Easy Celtic Guitar Solos	$15.99
00702156	3-Chord Rock	$12.99
00702220	Today's Country Hits	$12.99
00244654	Top Hits of 2017	$14.99
00283786	Top Hits of 2018	$14.99
00702294	Top Worship Hits	$15.99
00702255	VH1's 100 Greatest Hard Rock Songs	$29.99
00702175	VH1's 100 Greatest Songs of Rock and Roll	$27.99
00702253	Wicked	$12.99

ARTIST COLLECTIONS

00702267	AC/DC for Easy Guitar	$15.99
00702598	Adele for Easy Guitar	$15.99
00156221	Adele – 25	$16.99
00702040	Best of the Allman Brothers	$16.99
00702865	J.S. Bach for Easy Guitar	$14.99
00702169	Best of The Beach Boys	$12.99
00702292	The Beatles — 1	$19.99
00125796	Best of Chuck Berry	$15.99
00702201	The Essential Black Sabbath	$12.95
00702250	blink-182 — Greatest Hits	$16.99
02501615	Zac Brown Band — The Foundation	$19.99
02501621	Zac Brown Band — You Get What You Give	$16.99
00702043	Best of Johnny Cash	$16.99
00702090	Eric Clapton's Best	$12.99
00702086	Eric Clapton — from the Album Unplugged	$15.99
00702202	The Essential Eric Clapton	$15.99
00702053	Best of Patsy Cline	$15.99
00222697	Very Best of Coldplay – 2nd Edition	$14.99
00702229	The Very Best of Creedence Clearwater Revival	$15.99
00702145	Best of Jim Croce	$15.99
00702219	David Crowder*Band Collection	$12.95
00702278	Crosby, Stills & Nash	$12.99
14042809	Bob Dylan	$14.99
00702276	Fleetwood Mac — Easy Guitar Collection	$16.99
00139462	The Very Best of Grateful Dead	$15.99
00702136	Best of Merle Haggard	$14.99
00702227	Jimi Hendrix — Smash Hits	$19.99
00702288	Best of Hillsong United	$12.99
00702236	Best of Antonio Carlos Jobim	$15.99

00702245	Elton John — Greatest Hits 1970–2002	$17.99
00129855	Jack Johnson	$16.99
00702204	Robert Johnson	$12.99
00702234	Selections from Toby Keith — 35 Biggest Hits	$12.95
00702003	Kiss	$16.99
00110578	Best of Kutless	$12.99
00702216	Lynyrd Skynyrd	$16.99
00702182	The Essential Bob Marley	$14.99
00146081	Maroon 5	$14.99
00121925	Bruno Mars – Unorthodox Jukebox	$12.99
00702248	Paul McCartney — All the Best	$14.99
00702129	Songs of Sarah McLachlan	$12.95
00125484	The Best of MercyMe	$12.99
02501316	Metallica — Death Magnetic	$19.99
00702209	Steve Miller Band — Young Hearts (Greatest Hits)	$12.95
00124167	Jason Mraz	$15.99
00702096	Best of Nirvana	$15.99
00702211	The Offspring — Greatest Hits	$12.95
00138026	One Direction	$14.99
00702030	Best of Roy Orbison	$16.99
00702144	Best of Ozzy Osbourne	$14.99
00702279	Tom Petty	$12.99
00102911	Pink Floyd	$16.99
00702139	Elvis Country Favorites	$17.99
00702293	The Very Best of Prince	$16.99
00699415	Best of Queen for Guitar	$15.99
00109279	Best of R.E.M.	$14.99
00702208	Red Hot Chili Peppers — Greatest Hits	$16.99
00198960	The Rolling Stones	$16.99
00174793	The Very Best of Santana	$14.99
00702196	Best of Bob Seger	$15.99

00146046	Ed Sheeran	$17.99
00702252	Frank Sinatra — Nothing But the Best	$17.99
00702010	Best of Rod Stewart	$16.99
00702049	Best of George Strait	$14.99
00702259	Taylor Swift for Easy Guitar	$15.99
00254499	Taylor Swift – Easy Guitar Anthology	$19.99
00702260	Taylor Swift — Fearless	$14.99
00139727	Taylor Swift — 1989	$17.99
00115960	Taylor Swift — Red	$16.99
00253667	Taylor Swift — Reputation	$17.99
00702290	Taylor Swift — Speak Now	$16.99
00702223	Chris Tomlin—Arriving	$16.99
00232849	Chris Tomlin Collection – 2nd Edition	$12.95
00702226	Chris Tomlin — See the Morning	$12.95
00148643	Train	$14.99
00702427	U2 — 18 Singles	$16.99
00702108	Best of Stevie Ray Vaughan	$16.99
00279005	The Who	$14.99
00702123	Best of Hank Williams	$15.99
00194548	Best of John Williams	$14.99
00702111	Stevie Wonder — Guitar Collection	$9.95
00702228	Neil Young — Greatest Hits	$15.99
00119133	Neil Young — Harvest	$14.99

Prices, contents and availability subject to change without notice.

Visit Hal Leonard online at **halleonard.com**

0720
306